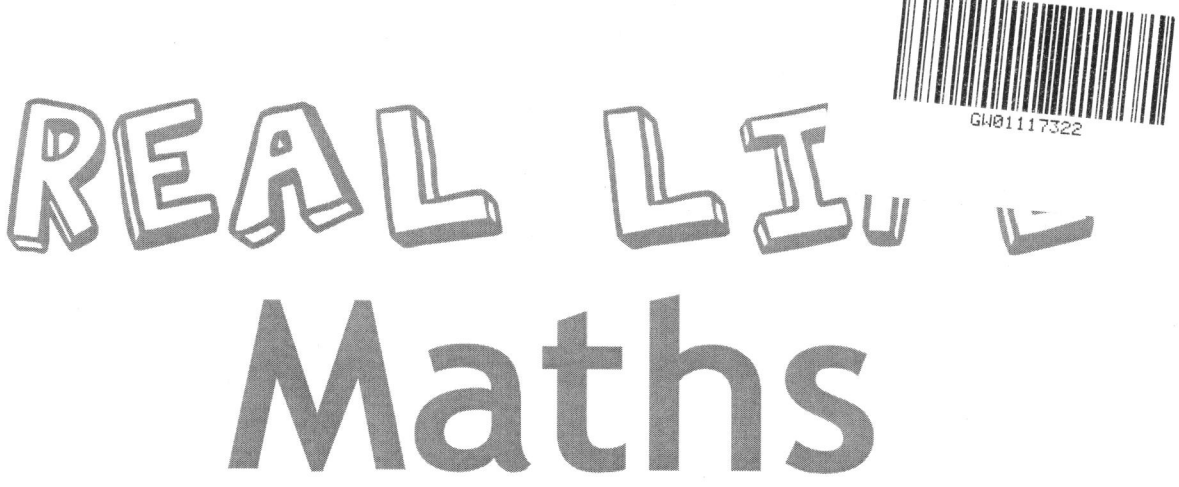

Maths

Book 1 - KS2/3

Exploring mathematical concepts in practical everyday ways.

David J. Cohen

Curriculum Concepts
comprehensive coverage

Real Life Maths – Book 1

ISBN 978 1 906373 90 0

Ordering Code – UK0384

Curriculum Concepts UK

The Old School

Upper High Street

Bedlinog

Mid-Glamorgan CF46 6SA

Email: orders@curriculumconcepts.co.uk

www.curriculumconcepts.co.uk

Copyright © Ready-Ed Publications - 2004

First published in United Kingdom, 2007

Revised and published Curriculum Concepts New Zealand, 2006

Copyright Information

This master may only be reproduced by the original purchaser for use with their class(es) only. The publisher prohibits the loaning or on selling of this master for the purpose of reproduction.

Written by David J. Cohen

Contents

Teachers' Notes – Rationale..4
Teachers' Notes – How to get the most from this book....................5
National Curriculum Links..6

Section 1: Making the Connections
Making the Connections - 1..7
Making the Connections - 2..8
Making the Connections: Your Assignments..................................9

Section 2: Maths Surveys
Maths Interview..10
Real Life Maths Survey One (a)...11
Real Life Maths Survey One (b)...12
Real Life Maths Survey Two (a)...13
Real Life Maths Survey Two (b)...14
Real Life Maths Survey Three (a)...15
Real Life Maths Survey Three (b)...16

Section 3: Maths in the News
Maths in the News - 1..17
Maths in the News - 2..18
Maths in the News: Your Assignments......................................19

Section 4: Maths in Advertising
Maths in Advertising - 1...20
Maths in Advertising - 2...21
Maths in Advertising: Your Assignments...................................22

Section 5: Taking a Holiday
Taking a Holiday - 1...23
Taking a Holiday - 2...24
Taking a Holiday - 3...25
Taking a Holiday - 4...26
Taking a Holiday - 5...27
Taking a Holiday - 6...28

Section 6: Planning a Holiday
Planning a Holiday: Your Assignments.....................................29
Planning a Holiday - 1...30
Planning a Holiday - 2: The Budget.......................................31
Planning a Holiday - 3...32

Section 7: Mobile Phone
Mobile Phones - 1..33
Mobile Phones - 2..34
Mobile Phones - 3..35
Mobile Phones - 4..36
Mobile Phones: Your Assignments..37
Reflection...38
Answers..39

Teachers' Notes

Rationale

Mathematics is all around us. We use mathematical processes from the time we get up in the morning until right before we go to sleep. An understanding of mathematical concepts helps students to arrive at school on time, order their lunch, purchase a CD, go to the movies, hire a DVD, deposit money into a bank account, pay for an excursion and even watch a favourite TV program.

Students also learn that adults need a firm understanding of mathematics to help them complete everyday tasks such as purchasing a home, shopping at the supermarket, sailing a boat, flying a plane, putting petrol in the car, cooking a meal, planning an overseas trip and paying the bills.

No matter where and even when people lived, mathematics has always helped solve everyday problems. The concept of mathematics wasn't invented by any one person or any one civilisation, but discovered by many people over time. Famous mathematicians in history, such as Pythagoras, Galileo and Archimedes, have paved the way for people to understand the way mathematical concepts work.

Even today, people are still discovering new ways that mathematics can help us to understand the world and the universe in which we live.

Reluctant maths students will benefit from the activities in this book as all activities are set in a real life context, allowing students to see the necessity for an understanding of mathematical skills in order to survive in the real world. Students will examine how mathematics is incorporated into their everyday "real life" world in a number of areas, such as using realistic examples that have great relevance for them.

Teachers' Notes

How to get the most from this book:

1. The initial activities in this book are designed to help students understand and appreciate the depth of maths in their everyday world. "Making Connections" is a great activity to start opening children's eyes to the real world of maths. The "Maths Surveys" are an excellent homework activity, where children can engage their family in the application and practicality of real life maths. The "Maths in News" and "Maths in Advertising" sections will help children read more into what they hear, read and see every day.

2. Each section contains a wide cross section of mathematical concepts for students to tackle and become immersed in. For example, this could include: **multiplication, adding, division, subtraction, rounding, analogue and digital clocks, graphing and interpreting data, identifying shapes, decimals, scales, location, maps, direction, working with temperatures, chance, graphing and interpreting data, area, estimation, prime numbers, identifying shapes, calendars and ordering.**

   The concepts covered are listed at the beginning of each section. These activities and questions also lend themselves to further discussion about the practical application of maths concepts.

3. There are many "open-ended" questions throughout the book. Students attempting open-ended questions for the first time often get confused and think they don't have enough information to successfully answer the question. To help understand the nature of these questions, write a sample question on the board and invite children to list the information that they think is missing. Students will soon discover that "could" type questions can include several different answers and subsequently, they have all the information they need in order to answer the question. Practising with open-ended questions will soon tune their thinking into a more flexible and deeper approach in finding different solutions to the same problem.

4. The activities in this book can be issued as weekly assignments or as a catalyst for working cooperatively in small groups and with partners.

5. After completion of the set assignment/s, children are encouraged to complete the Reflections form found on page 38. The reflection form is a self-analysis sheet designed to help children better understand their own work processes.

6. Research has shown that marking and providing feedback is more effective if given immediately after activities are completed. Allow children to explain how they arrived at answers. Often, there is more than just one way to arrive at an answer, however some methods are more efficient than others. By allowing pupils to share their method of working, the class will be exposed to alternative ways of reaching an answer.

National Curriculum Links

		Number; Number and algebra	Shape, space and measures	Handling data	Breadth of study
Section 1 Making the Connections	K2	1 a			
	K3				
Section 2 Maths Surveys	K2	1 a 3 a 4 a	1 a	1 c d e 2 a	1 a c d
	K3		1 a		
Section 3 Maths in the News	K2	1 a			
	K3				
Section 4 Maths in Advertising	K2	1 a			
	K3				
Section 5 Taking a Holiday	K2	1 b 3 a b 4 a	1 a	1 c d 2 a	1 a
	K3	1 b	1 a	1 a	
Section 6 Planning a Holiday	K2	1 b 3 a b 4 a	1 a	1 c d 2 a	1 a
	K3	1 b 3 m 4 a	1 a	1 a	
Section 7 Mobile Phone	K2	1 b 3 a b 4 a	1 a	1 c d 2 a	1 a
	K3	1 b 3 a b 4 a	1 a	1 a	

Making the Connections - 1

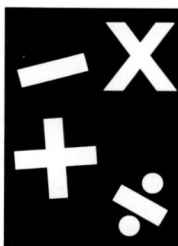

Background
Mathematics is the study of numbers and patterns. These patterns can be explained in sets of rules and then explored and examined by looking at the consequences of following those rules. People use mathematical concepts to solve problems and often use them without realising.

"Maths plays an important part in every person's daily life. It's not always immediately obvious, but maths is everywhere you look and even everywhere you don't look."

Demonstrating Your Understanding

You often hear teachers and parents say maths is all around us, but is this really true? Lets start with yourself. Think about your day and make a list of everything you have done that you think has involved the use of maths. When you have finished, share your list with others. You might want to add other ideas to your list after sharing.

Morning (AM)	Afternoon and Evening (PM)

Making the Connections - 2

Now that you have seen how maths is used in your life every day, let's have a look to see who else uses maths to help them though their day. Have a look at the occupations below and write down how you think maths is used in everyday job tasks. There is also room to add some of your own occupations.

Occupation	How they use mathematics
Plumber	• _____ • _____
Carpenter / Joiner	• _____ • _____
Builder	• _____ • _____
Painter	• _____ • _____
Accountant	• _____ • _____
Taxi driver	• _____ • _____
Journalist	• _____ • _____
Doctor	• _____ • _____
Web designer	• _____ • _____
Pilot	• _____ • _____
Retail shop assistant	• _____ • _____
Song writer	• _____ • _____
Computer programmer	• _____ • _____
_____	• _____ • _____
_____	• _____ • _____

Making the Connections: Your Assignments

Select from the following:

✱ Write a passage explaining the importance of maths in everyday life. Answer these questions:

- How is maths useful?
- Why is maths important?
- What jobs use maths?
- What things do you do that use maths?

✱ Make a PowerPoint presentation based on your findings about the importance of maths to people's everyday life.

✱ Hold a debate on the topic "Maths is not as important as it used to be". Select teams and a moderator. Allow the class to vote for who they think won the debate. Write up a report on the debate and include which side you support. Give reasons for your opinions.

✱ Write and perform a play about a selected famous mathematician such as Pythagoras, Galileo or Archimedes.

✱ Compile a list of films and books that involve a maths theme.
E.g. Books - The Code Book by Simon Singh, Three Little Pigs;
Films - A Beautiful Mind, Pi.
Write a film review from a mathematical point of view. Explain the basic mathematical concepts used in the film. You might like to look up some websites to help you with the review.

✱ Are there any jobs that you can think of that do not require the use of ANY mathematical concepts? Investigate and report back your findings.

✱ Use the interview sheet on the next page to establish the extent people rely on maths in their everyday lives. Discuss your findings with the class.

Maths Interview

Interview someone you know about the work that they do. Your "interviewee" may be a relative, an older friend or a next door neighbour. Write your responses on this form.

Name of person:

_____

1) What is your job title?

_____

_____

2) Job description – what does your job involve you doing?

_____

_____

_____

3) How important is maths in carrying out your job?

_____

Give examples of when and how you use maths in your daily job tasks:

_____

_____

_____

4) Do you use maths outside of your job?

_____

_____

Give some examples of when you do this:

_____

_____

_____

_____

5) Do you believe maths is an important subject to learn at school and why?

_____

_____

_____

Any additional comments or questions:

_____

_____

_____

_____

_____

_____

Follow-Up Activity:

Write a paragraph on your interview findings. Present to the class.

_____

_____

_____

_____

_____

Real Life Maths Survey 1a

Use your maths skills to find out how you and your family rely on maths understandings in your home every single day. Select a day of the week to complete this survey. Show how you arrived at the answer in the working out boxes. Remember, there is often more than one way of arriving at an answer. When you have finished, make a list of the mathematical concepts you used to help complete this survey.

Survey Day: _____ Name: _____ Class: _____

1) What is the address of your house?
   _____

2) What is your phone number?
   _____

3) How many people are there in your family?
   _____

4) What is the combined total age of everyone in your house?

   ► SHOW YOUR WORKING HERE:

   ANSWER

5) What is the average age of everyone in your house?

   ► SHOW YOUR WORKING HERE:

   ANSWER

8) What is the wattage capacity of your family's stereo speakers?
   _____

6) Order your family's height from smallest to tallest:
   _____
   _____
   _____
   _____
   _____
   _____

7) Order your family's length of hair from shortest to longest:
   _____
   _____
   _____
   _____
   _____
   _____

9) How many hours did your mum work today?

   ► SHOW YOUR WORKING HERE:

   ANSWER

10) How many hours were you awake yesterday?

    ► SHOW YOUR WORKING HERE:

    ANSWER

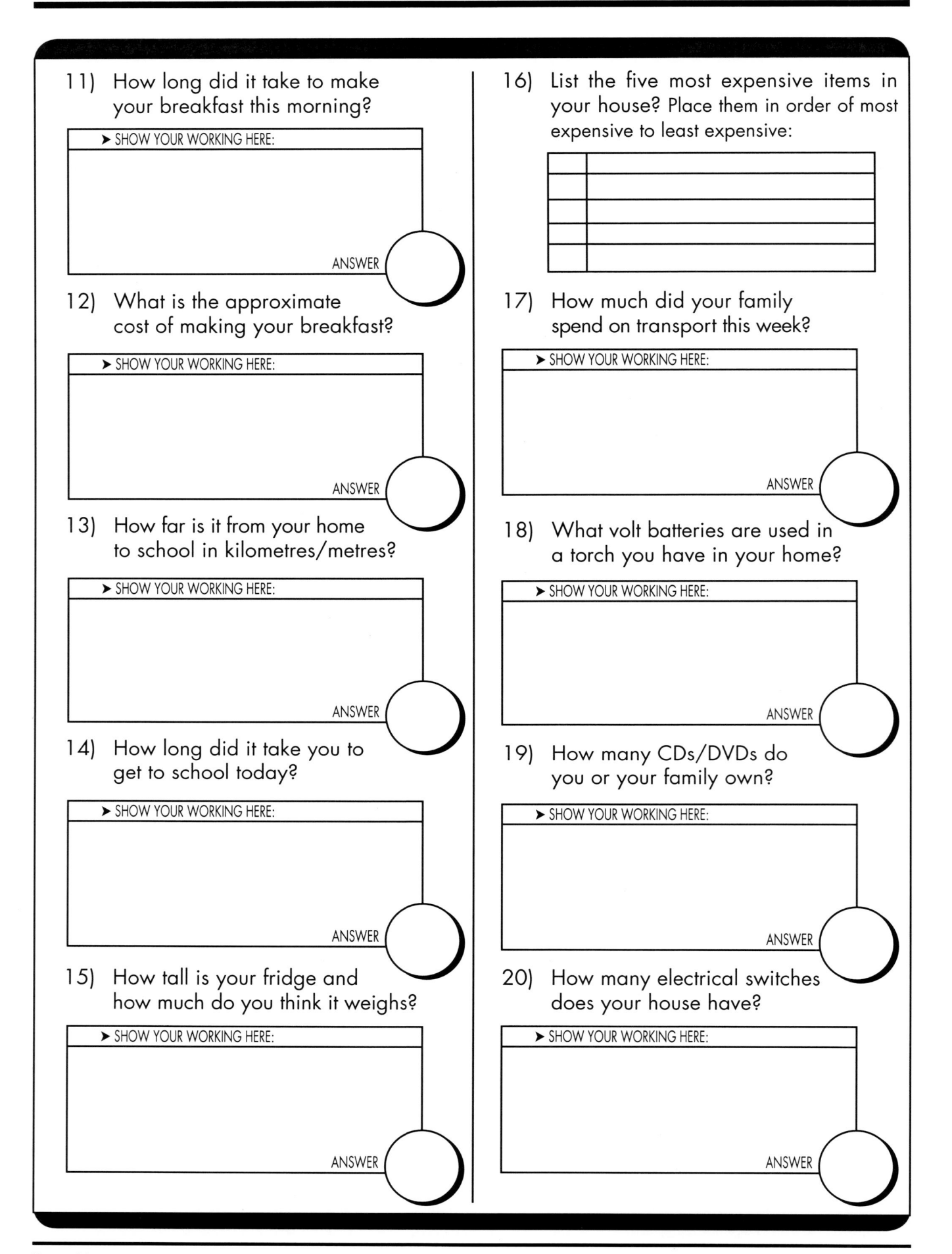

Real Life Maths Survey 1b

11) How long did it take to make your breakfast this morning?

> SHOW YOUR WORKING HERE:

ANSWER

12) What is the approximate cost of making your breakfast?

> SHOW YOUR WORKING HERE:

ANSWER

13) How far is it from your home to school in kilometres/metres?

> SHOW YOUR WORKING HERE:

ANSWER

14) How long did it take you to get to school today?

> SHOW YOUR WORKING HERE:

ANSWER

15) How tall is your fridge and how much do you think it weighs?

> SHOW YOUR WORKING HERE:

ANSWER

16) List the five most expensive items in your house? Place them in order of most expensive to least expensive:

17) How much did your family spend on transport this week?

> SHOW YOUR WORKING HERE:

ANSWER

18) What volt batteries are used in a torch you have in your home?

> SHOW YOUR WORKING HERE:

ANSWER

19) How many CDs/DVDs do you or your family own?

> SHOW YOUR WORKING HERE:

ANSWER

20) How many electrical switches does your house have?

> SHOW YOUR WORKING HERE:

ANSWER

Real Life Maths Survey 2a

Survey Day: _____   Name: _____   Class: _____

1) How many books do you own?

   > SHOW YOUR WORKING HERE:

   ANSWER

2) Approximately how much toothpaste is left in your house? (in grams)

   > SHOW YOUR WORKING HERE:

   ANSWER

3) What is the longest interval (in days) between birthdays that occur in your family.

   > SHOW YOUR WORKING HERE:

   ANSWER

4) How many houses are there in your street? _____. How is the sequence of the numbers on your side of the street ordered?

   _____

   _____

5) How many seconds does it take you to walk from your bedroom to the kitchen?

6) How many hours of TV does your family watch in a day?

   > SHOW YOUR WORKING HERE:

   ANSWER

7) a) How many advertisements are there in your favourite program?

   b) How many minutes are taken up by advertisements?

   > SHOW YOUR WORKING HERE:

   a)

   ANSWER

   b)

   ANSWER

8) What is the average length of each advertisement in your favourite show?

   > SHOW YOUR WORKING HERE:

   ANSWER

9) How many TV channels did you watch today and which channel did you watch for the greatest amount of time?

   _____

   _____

Real Life Maths Survey 2b

10) What percentage of the total number of rooms in your home are bedrooms?

> SHOW YOUR WORKING HERE:

ANSWER

11) Based on the area, order the rooms in your house from largest to smallest:

_____ _____
_____ _____
_____ _____
_____ _____
_____ _____

12) What is the area of the front OR back of your house? *Calculate your answer in square metres (m²).*

> SHOW YOUR WORKING HERE:

ANSWER

13) What shoe size does each person in your house wear? List.

NAME	SIZE
_____	_____
_____	_____
_____	_____
_____	_____
_____	_____

14) How many kilolitres of water did your family use today? *(Check your outside meter reading if you can or estimate).*

> SHOW YOUR WORKING HERE:

ANSWER

15) How much water do you use when you shower or bath? *(You may need to phone the water company to help you.)*

> SHOW YOUR WORKING HERE:

ANSWER

16) What is the capacity in litres of the petrol tank of your family or friends car? How much does it cost to fill up the tank?

> SHOW YOUR WORKING HERE:

ANSWER

17) What was the maximum temperature today?

_____

18) How many windows does your house have?

_____

19) Draw a floor plan of your house on a blank piece of paper.

Real Life Maths Survey 3a

Survey Day: _____   Name: _____   Class: _____

1) How many sets of knives and forks did you use today?

   > SHOW YOUR WORKING HERE:

   ANSWER

2) What radio station/s number did you listen to this day?

   _____

3) How many minutes of homework have you done so far this week?

   > SHOW YOUR WORKING HERE:

   ANSWER

4) How many points did your favourite sporting team win or lose by last weekend?

   > SHOW YOUR WORKING HERE:

   ANSWER

5) Approximately how many times in a day does your family turn the kitchen light switch on and off?

   > SHOW YOUR WORKING HERE:

   ANSWER

6) How many showers or baths does your family take in total in one week?

   > SHOW YOUR WORKING HERE:

   ANSWER

7) How many hours a week does your family spend cooking in the kitchen?

   > SHOW YOUR WORKING HERE:

   ANSWER

Real Life Maths Survey 3b

8) a) In a 24 hour period, what percentage of the time would you spend asleep?

b) What would this amount be per week?

► SHOW YOUR WORKING HERE:

a)

ANSWER

b)

ANSWER

9) What is the capacity in litres of your council rubbish bin?

► SHOW YOUR WORKING HERE:

ANSWER

10) Approximately how many times could you empty the kitchen bin into the council bin before it was full?

► SHOW YOUR WORKING HERE:

ANSWER

11) What maths did you use to help complete this survey?

_____

12) Write a paragraph about how you use maths every day at home.

_____
_____
_____
_____
_____
_____
_____
_____
_____
_____

Draw a picture of someone using mathematical concepts at home.

Maths in the News - 1

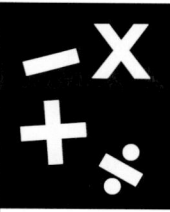

Background

Maths appears daily in news articles you see on television, the Internet and in newspapers and magazines. We don't usually think about the news and events as being mathematical, however, maths plays an important role in helping us understand our world.

For example, a write up about the football matches on the weekend is not that useful without knowing the final scores. An article about who won the election and by how much, relies on a lot of mathematical facts to get the message across. These stories use mathematical equations that everyone can understand, which is why it is important to learn about how maths can be used in our everyday world.

Demonstrate Your Understanding

Below and on the following page are some excerpts taken from articles that have appeared in the newspapers. Read them carefully and underline the maths concepts in each paragraph.

Order of the Phoenix, the latest 766-page Harry Potter adventure is set to break sales records. Supermarket chain Tesco sold an average number of 220 copies a minute in the first 24 hours, while bookstore WHSmith estimated a rate of eight sold per second. The book went on sale at the same time throughout the country, and at Waterstone's in central London, the boys and girls counted down the seconds to opening time... "Ten, nine, eight, seven." Fans have had to wait three years for this fifth instalment about the boy wizard Harry and his boarding school friends Ron and Hermione. A Tesco spokeswoman said that they sold 317,400 copies in the first 24 hours – compared to 42,000 copies of the fourth Harry Potter book, The Goblet of Fire, in its first week.

Roughly two-thirds of American college students play video games according to a survey completed last year by 1,162 college students on 27 campuses nationwide. Its results have a margin of error of 3 percentage points. About a third of those surveyed admitted playing computer games during class, while 65 per cent said they were regular or occasional game players. Most said they played in their rooms or parents' homes. Nearly 70 per cent of those questioned said they were in primary school when they first played video games.

Most Muslim children attend a madrassa for much of their childhood, learning how to lead good, upright Islamic lives, and an early lesson usually is that debt is undesirable and that you should go without what you can't afford to buy. Islam eschews interest-bearing loans on the basis that they create profit without work. But in a modern city like London, this is nearly impossible to achieve and many Muslims make monthly interest payments on houses, as the cost of purchasing a house outright is generally too great for most families to achieve when they most need accommodation, without the assistance of a mortgage.

The New Zealand dollar surged to $US60c today, a 5½ year high. At 5pm the New Zealand dollar was buying $US59.85c, up from $US59.46c on Friday, before climbing further to $US60.07c by 5.30pm. The Australian dollar rose to $US68.31c from Friday's $US68.19c.

After three years of construction and a price tag of more than $1 billion, the Borgata Hotel Casino & Spa opened its doors in ATLANTIC CITY, New Jersey at 11:30 pm Wednesday, three hours earlier than expected. The Borgata is the first new casino to open in Atlantic City since Trump Taj Mahal in 1990. The 2,002 rooms are wired for high-speed Internet access and the casino has 3,650 slot machines.

Maths in the News - 2

Read the news excerpts below. Underline the maths concepts in each paragraph.

United States "Consumer Reports" magazine reports that people may not be aware of the amount of the high level of caffeine in foods and drinks. Children need to be aware that excessive caffeine can leave them jittery and nervous. About 100 milligrams of caffeine in a day is enough. A can of Coke, a cup of caffeinated ice cream, and a half a cup of M&Ms each contain about 128 milligrams of caffeine.

The Arnold Schwarzenegger film, Terminator 3: Rise of the Machines, is expected to take in $US44 million ($A64.79 million) during its opening weekend. This is almost double the $US22.9 million ($A33.72 million) Legally Blonde 2: Red, White and Blonde is expected to earn in its opening weekend.

Bookies are currently offering odds of 2 to 1 that there will be snow in Edinburgh, Aberdeen & Glasgow this week and odds of 4 to 1 that snow will be felt in the major cities of England. Head of Markham and Sting of London, Delia Singh, says they normally see additional betting turnovers of about 12.55 when weather conditions make it suitable to offer gamblers such a flutter and she says they never see some punters betting except when weather outcomes are on offer.

The United Kingdom's biggest one-day pop event filled London's Hyde Park for the sixth annual event, which raises cash for the Prince of Wales' Trust. 100,000 eager pop fans saw chart-topping acts including Beyonce Knowles, Craig David and Atomic Kitten.

In Greater Manchester and Merseyside police officers have been warning drivers not to leave their car engines running while they keep nice and warm inside their house and wait for their windows to defrost on the cold mornings. Some 20 vehicles have been stolen in precisely these circumstances since Monday when the latest cold snap began. A few seconds of inattention by the owner is all a thief needs to affect a getaway when the engine is already running and the doors are unlocked said Chief Inspector Robin Banks of Greater Manchester police. As a double whammy for car owners struck by such a theft, cars may not be covered by their insurance if the vehicle is left unattended with the keys in the ignition and the engine running.

Coles Myer announced last month it had paid $94 million for 584 service stations throughout Australia, after drawn-out negotiations with oil refiner Shell. Woolworths has a 10 per cent share of the market, selling 46 million litres of petrol a week at its 280 Petrol Plus stations.

Weather forecast for south-east England: Dry with patchy cloud at times but often sunny. Gentle westerly winds. Warm. Maximum temperature 25 ° C (77 ° F). Tonight: A fine and dry evening and night but becoming increasingly cloudy later. Light winds. Mild. Minimum temperature 12 ° C (54 °F).

Up to 20% of Britain's energy needs could be generated using mountains of household rubbish that is currently wasted, a recent report has said. The Institute of Mechanical Engineers has claimed in its latest report, that the 300m tonnes of household rubbish - sufficient to fill the Albert Hall every two hours - produced each year could easily produce green power providing up to a fifth of the UK's electricity needs. This would help meet future Government targets for renewable energy generation, though environmentalists insist that the better option remains recycling. Whilst most of this rubbish is currently buried in landfills, new EU legislation requires a 50% reduction in landfill by 2013 so either recycling or power generation, or both must be considered. "We can't afford to do that any more, we're running out of space for landfills," said Mark Arbon, a visiting professor in energy systems at Newcastle University and author of the new report. Currently about 50 small-scale energy-from-waste plants operate in the UK compared with several thousand in countries such as Denmark and Germany.

Maths in the News: Your Assignments

Select from the following:

- Look through newspapers and magazines and cut out as many articles as you can that have maths in them or are maths related. Glue two or three (depending on size) of these articles into the space below and circle or underline the maths concepts. Make a note of the mathematics needed to understand the article.

- Make up your own news articles including as much maths as you can. Include concepts such as time, place, how many, how much and so on. Read them to a partner and then display your articles around the room.

Maths in Advertising - 1

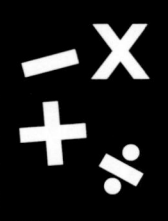

Background

Shopping is one of the most important things we are able to do to show we can take care of ourselves by meeting basic needs. Being able to go shopping, means we are responsible for our money and know how to use it to purchase goods. Sometimes we buy things we need such as food and clothes (needs). Other times we buy things we like to have, like a CD or watch (wants).

Businesses want you to spend money at their store and they usually advertise to encourage you to do so. We see advertisements all the time – in newspapers, magazines, on television and radio. There is also advertising on buses, trains and bill boards. Often advertisers offer specials and discounts to encouraged you to shop with them.

Demonstrate Your Understanding

Below are some sample paragraphs taken from advertisements that you might find in newspapers and magazines. Read them carefully and underline the mathematics in each advertisement. Discuss your understanding with a partner. Talk about what all the abbreviations mean.

CRAZY PETE'S PHONES

New Philips Fisio 820 mobile phone. Brings colour to your mobile world.

A large 256 colour display. Built-in modem, 19 ringer melodies. Specifications: 85 grams, 97 x 46 x 20mm, standby up to 4 hours 20 mins.

Product colour – Mars Red RRP: £100

Jock The Scot's Discounts

STORES IN EPPING, SOUTHLAND AND MT ERCIA

Tiny Digital MP3 player that easily fits in your pocket. Features: 32MB memory, Unit dimensions - 5.2cm (W) x 2.5cm (H) x 1.5cm (D), Play Back mode - Random / Repeat One or All, Equalizer - bass and treble, Lock switch - secures your player in play mode or locks the player in OFF state.

Now only £70. Be quick.

Computer Supermarket

The Travelmate 230 Series all-in-one multimedia notebook.

Features include: CPU mobile Intel® Celeron® processor 2.2 ghz, 1.44 MB fdd, 20 GB hdd, memory 128 MB, lithium ion battery, life up to 2.5 hours, 14.1" tft XGA colour LCD screen, twin stereo speakers, built-in 56kbps international fax/modem, 2 x usb 2.0 ports, CD-Rom 24 x CD-ROM drive. Weight: 3.0kg

Jock The Scot's Discounts

This CD system features a vertical CD player, and comes with a remote control. It has a AM/FM radio with 20 preset stations, and a built-in clock with calendar and alarm functions. Features: * CD System with PLL radio & multi-clock, temperature function, multi-clock with calendar and alarm function, the box measures 27cm in height, 47cm in width.

Was £369, now £319.

Maths in Advertising - 2

Read the advertisements below. Underline the maths concepts in each paragraph.

BLUE TICKETS
Ph. 131 123

Babies Proms - Popstars.
12 - 17 August;
Presenter: ABC Council

Babies Proms - Popstars lets you sing along to kid-friendly pop favourites with orchestral and rock accompaniment. The performances include demonstrations on how to sing and how to write a song. Babies Proms are the ever-popular kids program at the ABC Centre. Age: Suits 2-5 year olds. SEASON 12 - 17 August at 10am, 11am and 12 Noon. PRICE: All tickets £8 Child care, schools and parenting groups £6* (phone/counter bookings only). Teachers/carers free with group bookings (conditions apply).

GJ's Electronics

Hampden Road, Kingsley ph. 74589634
SONY G PROTECTION CD WALKMAN - DEJ361
CLEARANCE Price only for a limited time (while stocks last). Compact, stylish and featuring G-PROTECTION anti-skip mechanism for the ultimate in shock protection. With up to 40 hours playback, you will have hours of listening pleasure.

Price: £20
RRP: £29.50
Saving: £9.50

MASSIVE DVD CATALOGUE SALE - UP TO £20 OFF

The Massive DVD Catalogue Sale is now on! You can't beat this sale for mammoth savings on a huge range of your favourite titles. Over 250 titles have been sacrificed with savings of up to 75% off and DVDs starting from £4.95!

DOGGY HEAVEN

115 Albert Avenue,
West Park,
Third floor, ph 456 3849
Doggy Bowl £3 off, now only £8
Comes in a range of five exciting colours. Also comes with letters for labelling so that your dog will always know where his bowl is!

Art and Stuff
110 Carmichael Street, Bromley.
Open 10 to 5, seven days a week

Tube Kids Art. This Tube is an all in one tube! Contains: 1 x set of pencils, 1 x set of crayons, 2 x glitter glues, 1 x glue stick, 1 x safety scissors, 3 x stampers, 2 x packs stickers, 10 x coloured squares, 20 x fun foam.
Only £33.35

Grab all 3 July new release **Beanie Kids** at once for only **£36.00**
That's a 10% discount! They are as follows:

- Eco the Earth Fairy DOB: 12-Jan-2003. Star sign: Capricorn;
- Greta the Dutch Girl - Beanie Kid of the World DOB: 08-Jun-2002, Star sign: Gemini;
- Rattle the Tin Bear DOB: 03-Aug-2002 Star sign: Leo.

Strictly T-Shirts

£30.00
100% organic, generous fitting 180gsm cotton T-shirt.

Maths in Advertising: Your Assignments

Select from the following:

- Look through newspapers and magazines and cut out as many advertisements as you can that use maths to help sell their products. Glue as many as you can into the space below. Use a highlighter pen to note the maths used in each advertisement.

- On a separate sheet of paper make up your own advertisements, including as many mathematical ideas as you can, such as addresses, phone numbers, opening hours, specials, discounting and so on.

- Look carefully at the advertisements you see on television. Write down the maths that is used to explain the offers. Afterwards, write a script for your own advertisement using as many maths ideas as you can. With your friends, perform the advertisement for the class.

Taking a Holiday - 1

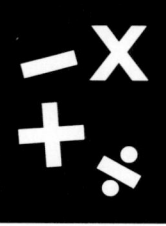

Background

People who travel on a holiday are called "tourists". People love travelling and enjoy the experience of seeing fantastic new places. Tourism is, in fact, the world's largest industry and currently the most popular international destination in the world is Europe, with the most visited country in the world being France.

When did you last go on a holiday? Do you realise how much maths is used to help you get there and enjoy yourself? You need to know how to read timetables and clocks, calculate travelling time and distances, handle money, change money into foreign currency, and pay for things like food, hotels, taxis and entry fees into tourist attractions. Maths is absolutely everywhere when you travel!

Maths Concepts Covered In This Topic

Multiplication, adding, division, subtraction, rounding, analogue and digital clocks, graphing and interpreting data, identifying shapes, decimals, scales, location, maps, direction, working with temperatures, chance, graphing and interpreting data, area, estimation, prime numbers, identifying shapes, calendars and ordering.

Demonstrate Your Understanding

1) Aunt May is meeting Uncle Tom at the airport. Aunt May's house is 15 kilometres away from the airport. How much time should she allow to get to the airport on time and what do you expect her average speed is likely to be? Explain.

   _____
   _____

2) Using an atlas or the Internet, find the approximate distances between the places below in kilometres. Be careful to take note of the scale if using maps. Assuming you can drive directly to your destination, estimate the amount of time needed to drive each distance if you average approximately 40 kilometres per hour.

ROAD TRIPS	APPROX DISTANCE (KM) (Round to nearest 10 km)	ESTIMATED TIME OF JOURNEY
London to Birmingham	160	approx. 4 hours
Reading to Derby	_____	_____
Dundee to Poole	_____	_____
Portsmouth to Luton	_____	_____
Cheltenham to Chelmsford	_____	_____
Harlow to Bath	_____	_____
Huddersfield to York	_____	_____
Redditch to Bracknell	_____	_____
Glasgow to Liverpool	_____	_____

Curriculum Concepts — Real Life Maths - Book 1

Taking a Holiday - 2

Complete the following. Show your working on the back of this page.

1) Our tour bus travelled from London to Bath in 3 hours 55 minutes. If the total distance travelled was 235 kilometres, what was the bus's average speed per hour?

   _____

2) A coach travelled a distance of 330 kilometres, in four hours. What was the average speed of the coach?

   _____

3) The bus driver announced to his passengers that they were about four hours away from Stonehenge. If they were averaging 75km/hour, approximately how many kilometres did they still need to travel?

   _____

4) The Thompson family phoned the airline to see what time Flight HK 184 was arriving from Hong Kong. The plane was initially due in at 5.59pm but was delayed by an hour and forty minutes. What is the new expected arrival time?

   _____

5) It is 2.40pm. Bill is boarding his plane for Paris in exactly 55 minutes. Draw this time and the scheduled boarding time on the analogue clock faces below.

6) If the time is 12.15pm and Paul is catching the bus for Machu Picchu at 12.47pm, how long does he have to wait?

   _____
   _____

7) The travel agent advised Diane that the only dates left for a flight to Croatia in the month of July were prime numbers. On what dates could she travel?

   _____
   _____

8) The captain on the plane announced to the passengers that the plane would be landing at Heathrow Airport in four and a half hours. What is another way of saying 'four and a half hours'?

   _____
   _____

9) Peter said he was taking a holiday in the snowfields to ski. List some destinations that he could be going to and state what month/s of the year it would have to be.

   _____

Taking a Holiday - 3

Complete the following:

1) While in the car, John looked out the window and counted 203 objects (of the same kind) before they arrived at the next town. What do you think he could be counting? Give five realistic examples.

   _____
   _____
   _____
   _____
   _____

2) Coming into land, Jackie noticed rectangular and circular shapes when she looked out of the plane window. What could she have been looking at?

   _____
   _____
   _____

3) The Anderson and Pyke families are meeting each other at Sunset Bay, 300 kilometres away from their home town. The Andersons left at 9am and travelled at 100 kilometres per hour. The Pyke family left at 9am also, but travelled at 90 kilometres an hour. However, the Pyke family knew a short cut that took 30km off the total distance. Who arrived first?

   _____
   _____
   _____

4) The Great Keppel Island Hotel is having a special offer – every fourth night of your stay is free! What is the average cost (per night) of staying eight nights if each night normally costs £200?

   _____
   _____

5) While on holiday, Boris heard the weather report say there was an 'even' chance of rain in the next 24 hours. What do you think this means?

   _____
   _____
   _____

6) What else do you think has a greater than even chance of happening? List at least five things.

   - _____
   - _____
   - _____
   - _____
   - _____

7) What do you think has a 'less than even' chance of happening? List at least five things.

   - _____
   - _____
   - _____
   - _____
   - _____

Taking a Holiday - 4

Complete the following:

1) According to the travel agent, the temperature for Fiji was hottest during January, February, and March. If the average temperature for the entire three months was 35°, what could the average temperatures be for EACH of those months?

   _____
   _____

2) At the snowfields, the average temperature over seven days was 5° Celsius. What could the temperature be for each day of the week to arrive at this average?

   _____
   _____

3) Julie is going on a 5-day holiday to the Greek Islands. The maximum weight permissible on bags checked in at the airport is 22 kilograms. Help Julie pack her bag so she does not exceed the weight requirement:

   Her shirts weigh 1.5kg each, her shorts weigh 1kg, her jeans weigh 1.5kg each, her jumpers weigh 1.2kg each, her bag of toiletries weigh 2kg, her reading books weigh 200g each, her computer laptop weighs 5.5kg, her diary weighs 500g, her hat weighs 100g and her suitcase itself weighs 4kg.

   What should she pack to keep under the limit?

   _____
   _____
   _____
   _____
   _____

4) Can you judge how much different things weigh? Complete this sentence so that it is accurate:

   A brick weighs more than a _____, which weighs more than a _____, which weighs more than a _____, which weighs more than a _____, which weighs more than a _____.

5) Distances between cities, towns and countries are usually measured in kilometres. What things do we usually measure in:

   metres _____
   _____
   _____

   centimetres _____
   _____
   _____

   millimetres _____
   _____
   _____

   acres _____
   _____
   _____

   square kilometres _____
   _____
   _____

Taking a Holiday - 5

Complete the following:

1) The travel agent needed to calculate the total distance and time travel for her client on this part of her world tour. Help her out:

Sydney to Auckland	= 2164 km	Flight Time: 3:35
Auckland to Honolulu	= 7061 km	Flight Time: 8:40
Honolulu to Los Angeles	= 4112 km	Flight Time: 5:12

   Total distance and time travel _____ _____

   Once you have calculated the total travel and distance time, draw this route on a map. Use an atlas and a blank sheet of paper.

FILL IN THE BLANKS

2) Convert these arrival and departure times to analogue and digital times:

	Flight	Gate	Analogue Time	Digital Time
Arriving from Singapore	412	5		0630
Departing to Adelaide	313	6	11.23am	
Arriving from Wellington	705	3		1304
Arriving from Kuala Lumpur	008	3	2.35pm	
Departing to Hong Kong	644	4		1458
Departing to London	548	6	6.14pm	
Arriving from Hawaii	987	2		1917
Arriving from LA	1311	3	10.03pm	

USE A SHEET OF GRAPH PAPER FOR THE FOLLOWING TWO QUESTIONS.

3) Construct a graph to present this information. You may choose from a bar graph, line graph or pie graph.

   Percentage of where international tourists travelled to in 2002:

   Africa – 4%, Americas – 17%, East Asia and the Pacific – 16%, Europe – 57%, Middle East – 3%, South Asia – 3%.

4) Construct a graph to present the information below.

   The top six most visited countries in the world in 2002:

   France – 76 million people, Spain – 50 million, United States – 45 million, Italy – 40 million, China – 33 million and United Kingdom – 23 million.

5) Look in an atlas or encyclopedia to find out the land mass of the countries listed in Question 4. Order them from smallest to largest.

Taking a Holiday - 6

Look at the Airline booking form below.

Answer the questions following.

One Way Only NZ$974 Return Only NZ$1800.

Air International Flight: 113   Departs: Auckland (AKL)   Arrives: Perth (PER)

9 July 2:00pm   9 July 5:40pm

Cabin class: Business (N), Economy (Y)   Meals: One   Distance: 5348 km   Stops: Non-stop   Duration: 7:40

---

1) How much can you save on a return trip? _____

2) The ticket says the total flight time is 7 hours and 40 minutes. However, the plane departs Auckland at 2pm and arrives in Perth at 5.40pm the same day. How is this possible?

   _____

   _____

3) What is the total distance travelled on a return trip from Auckland to Perth?

   _____

   _____

4) What is the total time travelled on a return trip from Auckland to Perth?

   _____

5) If it costs an additional 10% on the price to upgrade to Business Class, how much extra will need to be paid for a return flight?

   _____

   _____

6) How much would these flights be in pounds? _____

Planning a Holiday: Your Assignments

Select from the following:

- It is now possible to reserve airline tickets online using the Internet. Using the Internet, log onto a popular airline website.

  Have a go at seeing if you can reserve a seat. However, do this exercise with an adult or your teacher. DO NOT submit final confirmation or any credit card details.

- Design and make a train and carriage. What are the dimensions? How many people will it hold? Use cardboard, pop sticks, matchsticks, shoe boxes and other construction materials.

- On a piece of graph paper, design and draw an airport to scale. Show what the perimeter and area is for each part of the airport, such as the runways, control tower, airport lounge, etc. Use a legend to label each part of the airport.

- Select a destination to which you would like to take a holiday. You may travel anywhere around the world, and select any style of accommodation and transport from camping to a camper van, to flying from hotel to hotel.

Create a plan using the points below as a guide:

- *There are quite a few things to consider such as: What you might see and do in each place. How much money will you need? How are you going to pay for the trip? How many people are coming with you? What will you need to take with you? What will you need to buy? When is the best time to go (some days and times are more economical than others)?*

- *You will also need to consider where you are going to find the information you need to use in planning your trip. The most obvious place to start is the Internet, however there are other sources for you to consider such as travel agents and magazines, approaching the government, commercial and community organisations, talking on the phone, sending e-mails and/or collecting information through personal interviews.*

- *On the following page is a sample overview sheet to help begin your planning. Your teacher may agree to alternative and additional ways in which to present this assignment, such as: a written report, PowerPoint presentation, EXCEL, live website or through another multimedia format.*

  You may also want to include copies of advertisement, flyers, timetables, itineraries, maps and diagrams.

Planning a Holiday - 1

Overview

Destination: _____

Number of friends/family accompanying you: _____
_____

Will any expenses be shared? If so, what?
_____
_____

Total number of days and nights:
_____

Travel

Exact date of departure and why:
_____
_____

Total distance (in km) from your leaving point:
_____
_____

Total time in travelling to your destination:
_____

Selected method of travel:
_____

Reason for this method:
_____
_____

Include: •Itinerary •Timetables (e.g. bus) •Map

Accommodation

Accommodation arrangements *(e.g. how many beds, sizes of rooms, required facilities, proximity to attractions, etc.).*
_____

Accommodation cont.
_____
_____
_____
_____

Include: •Advertisements •Floor Plans •Map

Recreational Activities

Planned recreational activities *(types of activities, how many people involved, equipment needed, estimated costs, etc.).*
_____
_____
_____
_____
_____
_____

Include: •Advertisements •Flyers

Establishing the Cost

What will you need for the trip? What do you already own? What will you need to buy and what is the expected cost?

You will also need to consider the total number of days you will be away and if any expenses are going to be shared. If this is the case then you need to divide the costs evenly or as agreed. Show working out on the back of this page.

Income and Expenses

Establish the total expenses required to pay for your trip.

Now, follow the budget plan on pages 31 and 32.

Planning a Holiday - 2: The Budget

BUDGET		
Expenses	Workings (Estimate)	Final Cost
TRAVEL		
Air		
Car		
Taxis		
Bus		
Train		
Ship		
Other		
COMMUNICATION		
Phone cards		
Mobile telephone		
Landline calls		
Internet café		
Postcards/postage		
Other		
ACCOMMODATION		
Caravan park		
Backpackers		
Hotel		
Other		
FOOD/DRINKS		
Breakfast		
Lunch		
Dinner		
Drinks		
CLOTHING/SHOES		
Clothing		
Shoes		
Accessories		
TOTAL COST		

Planning a Holiday - 3

Complete the following questions based on your budget entries.
Show your working for each question.

1) In exactly how many days time will you leave for your holiday?
   _____

2) Place in numerical order the most expensive component of the trip to the least:
   _____
   _____
   _____

3) How can you reduce costs by 10%? Show your workings.
   _____
   _____
   _____

4) How many litres of fuel are needed for the trip? Based on today's price of petrol, what will the cost be?
   _____
   _____

5) What is the most efficient and cost effective method of transport?
   _____
   _____

6) Travel agents charge a commission for any bookings they make. Investigate what the commission rates are in the travel industry.

   Calculate the total amount of commissions earned by travel agents from your bookings.
   _____
   _____
   _____
   _____

Mobile Phones - 1

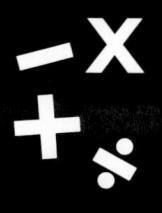

Background

Although digital wireless technology dates back to the 1940s, mobile telephones have only been readily available since the early 1990s. Businesses were the first to use mobile phones, making appointments and speaking to clients at any time or place.

First (1G) and Second Generation (2G) phones expanded the use of mobiles around the world as they became smaller, cheaper to buy and easier to operate. The cost of a mobile phone came within the reach of most people by the end of the 1990s. People from all walks of life wanted to own a mobile phone. In 2003 alone, sales around the world were about half a billion cell phones.

For peace of mind, parents may buy their children a mobile phone in case of emergencies. However, children see mobiles more as a social tool to keep in contact with friends. Text messaging has bought in a new and popular way for people to communicate.

In 2003, Third Generation (3G) phones were released. Third Generation mobiles can download videos, send e-mail, surf the Internet and send live video and picture messaging. Fourth Generation (4G) phones are due for release in 2010 and will allow even faster downloading of entire movies and CDs with high quality pictures and sound.

Maths Concepts Covered In This Topic

Multiplication, adding, division, subtraction, rounding, analogue and digital clocks, graphing and interpreting data, identifying shapes, decimals, scales, maps, symmetry, data and 3D construction.

Demonstrate Your Understanding

1) Mobile phones are usually bought on a 'plan'. A plan is like a contract where the purchaser agrees to pay for the phone over time – usually 18 or 24 months.

Calculate the monthly cost of these plans:

i) 24 month contract of £1068 total cost for the phone, including £20 worth of calls per month, plus £100 upfront connection fee: _____

ii) 24 month contract of £768 total cost for the phone, including £15 worth of calls per month, plus £100 upfront connection fee: _____

iii) 12 month contract of £288 total cost for the phone, including £10 worth of calls per month, plus £0 upfront connection fee: _____

iv) 12 month contract of £300 total cost for the phone, including £10 worth of calls per month, plus £0 upfront connection fee: _____

Mobile Phones - 2

1) Calculate the total cost of these plans:

   a] £32 per month for 24 months, including £10 worth of calls per month plus £50 connection fee: _____

   b] £50 per month for 24 months, including £20 worth of calls per month plus £100 connection fee: _____

   c] £32 per month for 12 months, including £20 worth of calls per month plus £50 connection fee: _____

   d] £100 per month for 12 months, including £30 worth of calls per month plus £0 connection fee: _____

2) Look at this company comparison grid and then answer the questions after.

Network	Offer
Amazing Phone Network	• 30p per 30 second block, plus 10p connection fee between 7am to 7pm. • After 7pm till 7am free for the first 10 minutes to any other Amazing Phone Network phone, then 22p for 10 minutes thereafter. No connection fee applies. • After 7pm till 7am free for the first 5 minutes to any other Network, then 30p per minute thereafter. 30p connection fee applies.
Tele Connex Network	• 10p flat rate per min 24 hours a day, plus 30p connection fee.
Freedom Network	• Standard rates 30p per minute. No connection fee. • 1p per minute between 8pm and 7am any night, plus 50p connection fee. Standard rates apply after 10 minutes. • Standard rates are 30p for seconds.

   a] If you made all your phone calls to a friend (not on the same network as you) at 8.30 pm every night for 6 minutes, which network would you join to make the cheapest calls? _____

   b] What is the difference in cost between the most expensive network and the least expensive? _____

   c] Which network would work out to be cheapest if most of your calls are less than five minutes in duration and are made before 7pm? _____

   d] If you wanted to join a network, which would you choose and why? To answer this question you will need to firstly establish how many calls you would make and when. _____

Mobile Phones - 3

1) Draw the time of the day that you think most people make their phone calls. Express this time on the digital and analogue clockfaces below.

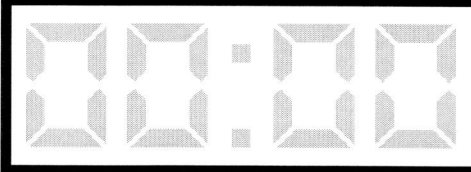

2) Yesterday Dad made seven calls to Mum using his mobile phone. What was the total amount of time spent on these conversations if the calls took place between the following times?

   Call Time   Duration

   8.09 to 8.17   _____

   11.37 to 1.13   _____

   2.29 to 2.31   _____

   4.59 to 5.41   _____

   TOTAL TIME   _____

3) When turning on a phone mobile, you need to key in a 4-digit security code. Make up your own four-digit PIN and explain why your code is easy to remember.

   _____

4) Mobile phones are in the shape of a rectangular prism. List two other objects that have this shape.

   _____

5) Make a list of objects around your classroom that are shaped like a:

   Cylinder _____

   Triangular prism _____

   _____

   Cone _____

   _____

   Sphere _____

   _____

6) Karen made the following long distance calls on her mobile during the month of June.

NUMBER	DURATION	TIME
CALL 1 - 0234 567 890	1 MIN 12 SEC	PEAK
CALL 2 - 1783 988 802	45 SEC	PEAK
CALL 3 - 0234 567 890	4 MIN 38 SEC	OFF PEAK
CALL 4 - 3242 989 000	3 MIN 1 SEC	PEAK
CALL 5 - 5432 094 892	13 MIN 29 SEC	OFF PEAK

   Work out the total cost of these calls based on the rates below:

   LONG DISTANCE CALL RATES:
   PEAK - 29p PER 30 SECONDS
   OFF-PEAK - 15p PER 30 SECONDS

   Remember that calls are billed in 30 second blocks so if the time is less than 30 seconds, it is still billed for that amount, i.e. speaking for 9 seconds would cost the same as speaking for 30 seconds. Speaking for 31 seconds would result in the charge for a full minute.

   _____

   _____

   _____

Mobile Phones - 4

Complete the following problems:

1) Josie's phone was always 'dropping out'. This meant her phone stopped working and she could no longer hear the person she was talking to. What are some possible reasons why mobile phones 'drop out'?

_____

_____

_____

_____

2 **Symmetry**

Complete this picture of a mobile phone.

Mobile Phones: Your Assignments

Select from the following:

- Mobile Phone Survey: Ask people from your class questions about mobile phones and present your findings in a report. You may want to graph or use tables to present your information. Write a paragraph about what you discovered from your data collection.

- Design and make a gift box that will fit a mobile phone. You will need to calculate the total size (volume) of the phone first. Make the package as realistic as possible by including details of the phone, such as features and brand details.

- Design and construct your own mobile phone. You may want to use matchsticks, popsticks or a cardboard net to construct a 3D model. Make a list of the phone features and show the cost details involved in buying the phone outright or using a plan. Explain in detail the total costs of the phone.

- A mobile phone company has asked you to re-design their store for them. Draw a bird's eye design to scale. Include a legend and direction.

    Before you start, conduct some research by visiting mobile phone stores, paying attention to the layout. Clearly label your diagram and explain the reasons for your placement of objects.

- The mobile phone market is very competitive. Companies market their products very aggressively which is good news for the consumer as it means you can look out for the best deal.

Compile a report detailing the most cost-effective way to own your own mobile phone for a 24-month period.

You will need to include:

- *The purpose of owning the phone (e.g. emergencies, social, family, text messaging, video calls, etc.);*
- *How many calls you expect to make each month;*
- *The total cost of owning a phone for 24 months. You will need to investigate and show the option of buying the phone outright versus signing on for a 24-month contract. Be careful to read the "fine print". Examine what the fine print means to your total cost;*
- *Explain how you are going to pay for the phone – this includes initial connection costs and on-going monthly charges;*
- *Include pamphlets and/or advertisements in your final presentation.*

Reflection

Name: _____ Class: _____ Date: _____

Assignment Task: _____

When you have finished your assignment answer these questions:

1) What mathematics did you use for this assignment?
   _____
   _____

2) Do you feel your knowledge of maths concepts has improved? If so, how?
   _____
   _____

3) Who else did you work with on these assignments and activities?
   _____
   _____

4) What part of this assignment did you enjoy the most?
   _____
   _____

5) What part of this assignment did you find the most challenging?
   _____
   _____

6) What would you do better or differently next time?
   _____
   _____
   _____

Additional comments: _____
   _____
   _____

Answers

Making the Connections (Pages 7–9):

Answers will vary.

Maths Interview (Page 10):

Answers will vary.

Real Life Maths Surveys (Pages 11-16):

Answers will vary.

Maths in the News (Pages 17-19):

Answers will vary – Check passages.

Maths in Advertising (Pages 20-22):

Answers will vary.

Taking a Holiday - 1 (Page 23):

1) Answers will vary;
2) Check Table: (Distances calculated using **www.distance calculator.globefeed.com/uk**
   Students approximations will probably differ to those given below based on where students have sourced the travel information. Check that students have understood the estimation process and ask them to take into consideration that durations can vary depending on the traffic congestion and road quality.

London to Birmingham	160 km	approx. 4 hours
Reading to Derby	170 km	approx. 4 hours 15 mins
Dundee to Poole	650 km	approx. 16 hours 15 mins
Portsmouth to Luton	130 km	approx. 3 hours 15 mins
Chettenham to Chelmsford	180 km	approx. 4 hours 30 mins
Harlow to Bath	180 km	approx. 4 hours 30 mins
Huddersfield to York	60 km	approx. 1 hour 30 mins
Redditch to Bracknell	130 km	approx. 3 hours 15 mins
Glasgow to Liverpool	280 km	approx. 7 hours

Taking a Holiday - 2 (Page 24):

1) 60 kph
2) 82.5 km / hour
3) Approximately 300 km
4) 7.39pm
5) 3.35pm
6) 32 minutes
7) 2nd, 3rd, 5th, 7th, 11th, 13th, 17th, 19th, 23rd, 29th, 31st
8) Answers will vary but should include:
   270 minutes, 16 200 seconds, 18.75% of the day, 4.5 hours, 4 hours and 30 minutes
9) Answers will vary.

Taking a Holiday - 3 (Page 25):

1) Answers will vary
2) Answers will vary but could include: water tank, running tracks, lakes, gardens, houses (buildings)
3) They arrived at the same time (12 noon)
4) £150
5) Answers will vary but can reflect on 50% chance of rainfall over the next day
6) Answers will vary but may include: the sun coming up, water coming out of a tap, the radio working, the trains working
7) Answers will vary but may include: able to stay awake all night, doubling your weekly allowance, beating dad in a running race, school closing on a weekday.

Taking a Holiday - 4 (Page 26):
1) Answers will vary but may include 35° for each month or could be a combination such as Jan - 36, Feb - 38, Mar - 31
2) Answers will vary
3) Answers will vary but must not total more than 22kg and should include the weight of the suitcase (4kg)
4) Answers will vary
5) Answers will vary

Taking a Holiday - 5 (Page 27):
1) Total distance 1337 km. Total travel time 17 hours and 27 mins
2) Check Table:

Arriving from Singapore	412	5	6.30am	0630
Departing to Adelaide	313	6	11.23am	1123
Arriving from Cairns	705	3	1.04pm	1304
Arriving from Wellington	008	3	2.35pm	1435
Departing to Hong Kong	644	4	2.58pm	14.58
Departing to London	548	6	6.14pm	1814
Arriving from Hawaii	987	2	7.17pm	1917
Arriving from LA	1311	3	10.03pm	2203

3) Answers will vary, e.g. Check bar graph, pie graph, pictograph, line graph, etc.
4) Answers will vary, e.g. bar graph, pie graph, pictograph, line graph, etc.
5) United Kingdom (244,755 km^2), Italy (301,245 km^2), Spain (504,880 km^2), France (543,965 km^2), United States (936,3130 km^2), China (959,700 km^2).

Taking a Holiday - 6 (Page 28):
1) NZ$148
2) Time zones
3) 10,696 km
4) 15 hours 20 minutes
5) NZ$180
6) Answers will vary depending on exchange rate.

Planning a Holiday (Pages 29-32):
Answers will vary.

Mobile Phones - 1 (Page 33):
1) a] £44.50. Note: As the connection fee is paid upfront, it's not a monthly expense
   b] £32. Note: As the connection fee is paid upfront, it's not a monthly expense
   c] £24
   d] £25

Mobile Phones - 2 (Page 34):
1) £818; £1300; £434; £1200
2) a) Freedom Network (Amazing 60p, TeleConnex 90p, Freedom 56p)
   b) 34p
   c) TeleConnex Network
   d) Answers will vary

Mobile Phones - 3 (Page 35):
1) Answers will vary
2) 146 minutes in total;
3) Answers will vary
4) Answers will vary
5) Answers will vary
6) £9.03. Individual calls: 87p, 58p, £1.50, £2.03, £4.05

Mobile Phones - 4 (Page 36):
1) Answers will vary; e.g. size of cities and town centres, faulty phone. These can all effect the phone reception
2) Check diagram for symmetry.